AN ILLUSTRATE IT YOURSELF BOOK

G.G.Wallace

 www.trafford.com

North America & international
toll-free: 1 888 232 4444 (USA & Canada)
phone: 250 383 6864 ♦ fax: 812 355 4082

Contents

Cammie's Secret

"Mummy, Mummy, do I have to go?" asked Cameron.

"Yes Cammie," said Mummy. "You have to go and it will be fine. You'll see."

It was Sunday night and Cammie had just said his prayers. But he did not want to go to bed because when he woke up it would be Monday and his first day at school. Cammie was afraid. He did NOT want to go to school. Mummy kissed Cammie good-night and softly tip-toed away. Cammie's eyes closed and he began to dream.

In his dream Cammie was no longer a little boy. He was a beautiful yellow bird. NOW HE DID NOT HAVE TO GO TO SCHOOL. He flew to the window ledge.

"Good morning sky! Good morning sun! It is Monday and I do NOT HAVE TO GO TO SCHOOL!"

But he was lonely. "Where are all the other birds?" he asked. He flew over the garden and down the street. He flew past his friend Kenny's house but Kenny was not home. Kenny had gone to school.

Then far off down the street he saw some birds perched high on a wire. One, two, three, four, five. There were so many birds he could not count all of them.

"Hello," he said. "May I sit with you?"

"Yes, yes," answered the birds. They were chirping happily.

"Why are you so happy?" he asked.

"We are happy because it is Monday and time for school," said a pretty red bird.

"At song time Miss Grant will play the piano and the children will sing like us," said an orange bird.

"At playtime the children will flap their arms and pretend to fly like us," said a little brown bird.

"And when they go back inside they will colour and paint beautiful birds of many colours," chirped a plain black bird. "The children make us happy!"

The next morning Cammie awoke. He was not a bird. He was still a little boy. It was still Monday and he still had to go to school. But he was not afraid. He wanted to go to school so that he could sing like a bird. He wanted to flap his arms and pretend to fly like a bird. He wanted to paint beautiful birds. But best of all Cammie had a secret. He knew why the birds outside his classroom window would be chirping so gaily.

It's Raining

"Rain, rain, go away . . . come again another day . . ." It was raining and Sammy was sad. It had been raining all morning and he could not go out to play. His friends could not come out to play with him because of the rain. Even his dog Buffy did not want to play anymore. It was a grey, wet, sad day. As Sammy sat at the window watching the raindrops and listening to the pitter patter against the glass, his eyes slowly closed. The rain fell softly against the window pane.

But now Sammy heard a new song. "Rain rain, without the sun . . . even rain can bring some fun . . ."

"Fun?" asked Sammy. "How can the rain be fun?" Then Sammy heard another new sound. It was laughter, but where was it coming from? Sammy saw a flash of bright yellow in the garden. The flowers were laughing.

The flowers were bobbing their heads happily back and forth. The rain was tickling them as it fell onto their yellow petals and under their bright green leaves.

In the bird bath a little blue bird chirped happily as he flapped his wings up and down and up and down. He was laughing too as he swam back and forth, round and round, in his newly filled swimming pool.

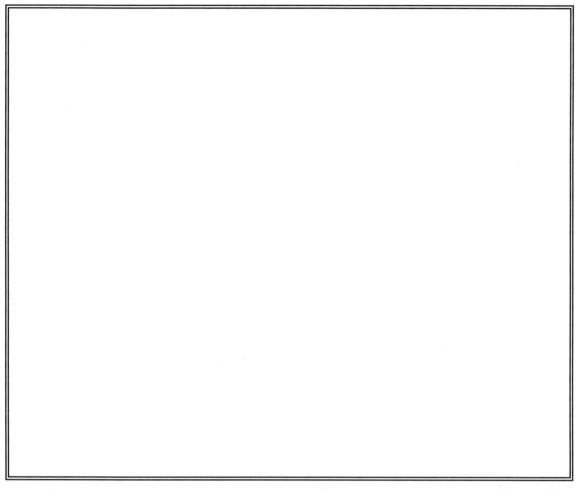

Even the clouds were having fun as they puffed up with rain, blowing gently into many new and different shapes as they chased each other across the sky.

The raindrops laughed too as they drew pretty pictures on Sammy's window with squiggly lines from top to bottom. Oh yes, the rain was fun for everyone.

Sammy's eyes slowly opened. The yellow flower heads were still. The bird had flown away, the window was dry, and the bright yellow sun had started to shine.

"The rain really was fun," thought Sammy. "But now it is taking its nap just like I did."

The Twins Learn to Share

"What a racket! What a noise! Why are you two children squabbling and being so grouchy?" Mummy asked the twins. "You are three years old!" she scolded.

"I want to play with the red fire engine," said Donnie.

"I had it first!" argued Ronnie.

"Boys, boys," said Mummy sternly, "this is poor behavior. There is a better way to play. It is called SHARING."

"Ronnie, you may play with the red fire engine. Donnie, why don't you play with the blocks? Maybe you could build a big fire station for the truck. When you are finished you can trade. Now remember boys, you must try your best to SHARE EVERYTHING."

Mummy went to wash the dishes and the boys began to play nicely. They shared the big red fire engine and they shared the blocks. Together they pretended to put out a big fire and save all of the people.

As they played, Ronnie began to feel warm all over. Donnie felt very warm too.

"It must be from all our hard work putting out the fire," they said. But something else was happening.

"Ronnie," said Donnie, "you have little red spots on you!"

"So do you," said Ronnie. "You have LOTS OF SPOTS!"

"Mummy, Mummy," shouted the boys. "Look at us. We feel warm all over and we have spots."

"Oh no," said Mummy. "It is the measles and it is on both of you. Did both of you have to get the measles?"

Donnie looked at Ronnie. Ronnie looked at Donnie. Then both boys looked at Mummy and they started to laugh.

"Mummy, Mummy," they giggled. "We are doing what you told us to do. WE ARE SHARING EVERYTHING!"

Milton Mouse Runs Away

(A story from the Bahamas)

"Milton, Milton," called Mummy Mouse. "Where are you? It is time for you to clean your room."

But Milton Mouse was nowhere to be found. Milton did not want to do his share of the work and he had run away from his home in a big warehouse on Arawak Cay, in Nassau, Bahamas. He ran across the road and over the rocks to the water's edge.

"Milton," called Susie Seagull, "where are you going?" But Milton did not answer. He jumped right off of a big rock onto a sea grape leaf floating on the clear aquamarine water. And away he floated towards Paradise Island Bridge. He was off to see the world.

Meantime, back on Arawak Cay, Milton was missing. Daddy Mouse called a meeting of all the birds and animals who lived near their house.

"Milton is missing," he said. "Has anyone seen Milton?"

Susie Seagull told Daddy Mouse how she had seen Milton floating on the sea grape leaf towards Paradise Island Bridge.

"Quick! Quick!" said Daddy Mouse. "We must hurry. Milton cannot swim."

"I'll help," called Gary Grouper from the shoreline, and off he swam flashing through the waves. His tail swished back and forth guiding him through the harbor towards the bridge. And then he heard a tiny sound. It was Milton on the sea grape leaf.

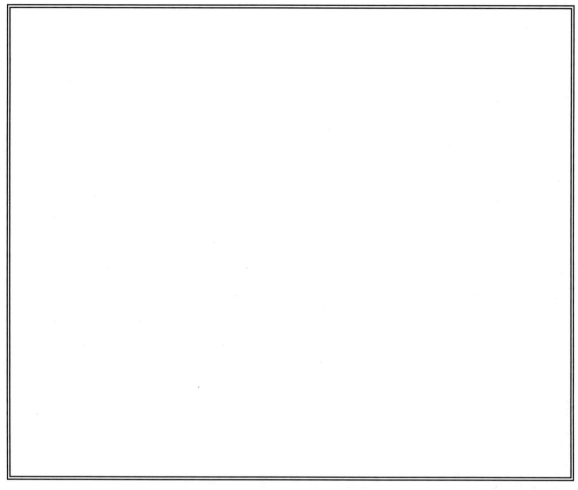

"Help, help," squeaked Milton. "I am going too far and I cannot swim. Help! Help!"

Gary Grouper nudged the leaf gently with his snout.

"Jump on my back Milton and hang on tight. I will take you home."

Soon Milton was back at Arawak Cay.

"Oh Milton," said Mummy Mouse. "I am so happy that you are safe. But you have been very naughty. You should not have run away. Now you must do extra chores for a week."

But this time Milton was happy to do the work because he was even happier to be safely home.

Naughty Jerome

Jerome was a very naughty little boy. When his mummy bought him a new book from the big book store downtown he sat right down and tore the pages out.

"You are a very naughty boy," said his mummy. But Jerome did not care.

When Mummy took Jerome to the nearby park to play on the swings he pulled up handfuls of beautiful flowers.

"You are a very naughty little boy," said the groundskeeper. But Jerome did not care.

When Jerome went into the shop with Mummy to buy bread, he grabbed an orange from the fruit section and began to eat it.

"You are a very naughty little boy," said the shopkeeper. But Jerome didn't care. Everyone cared except Jerome. It was not right for such a little boy to be so naughty.

Then a happy little fly who had been watching Jerome all morning had an idea.

"I will play a trick on Jerome," he thought. "I will help him not to be so naughty."

So every time Jerome went to do something naughty the little fly buzzed in Jerome's ear.

"Do not be so naughty," whispered the little fly.

When Jerome went to pull the cat's tail he buzzed in his ear and Jerome had to leave the cat alone to try to swat the fly.

When Jerome bent down to pick up a rock to throw at a bird the little fly buzzed in his ear.

"Do not be so naughty," whispered the little fly. Jerome dropped the rock to try to swat the fly. Every time Jerome tried to be naughty the fly buzzed in his ear. "Do not be so naughty. Do not be so naughty."

On and on it went, day after day. Every time Jerome was about to do something naughty that little fly was right there to buzz in his ear and stop Jerome from being a naughty boy.

Soon Mummy noticed that Jerome was not being so naughty.

"What a good boy you are," she said. "Come and let me give you a big hug and a big kiss."

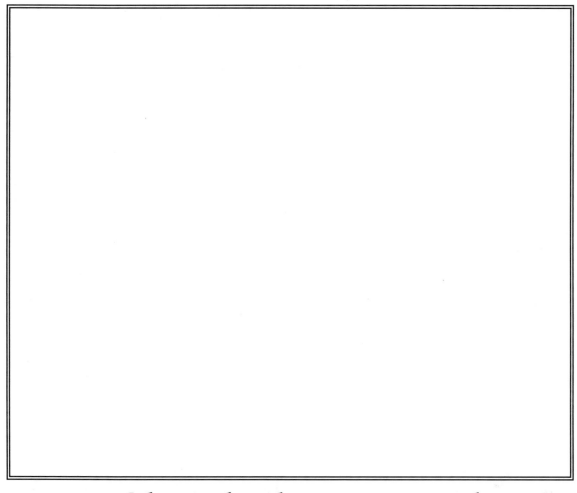

Jerome felt good. When Mummy and Jerome went to the little shop on the corner Jerome was no longer naughty.

"What a good boy you are," said the shopkeeper. "Here is a candy for such a good boy."

And Jerome felt good.

One day the little fly did NOT buzz in Jerome's ear at all. It was time for Jerome to be a good boy all by himself. And that is exactly what he did. Jerome was no longer naughty so Mummy bought her good boy a new book. Jerome sat right down and turned the pages very carefully!

Who's Singing?

"Jamie . . . Jamie . . . are you ready for bed yet?" called Mummy from the bottom of the steps.

"Just about," answered Jamie from behind the bathroom door.

"And remember to brush your teeth," called Mummy. "That chocolate cake you ate for dessert will give you cavities if you don't brush."

"O.K. Mummy," answered Jamie. But he was not brushing his teeth. He was playing with his toy boat in the sink.

Soon Mummy came upstairs and sat on the edge of Jamie's bed. After a story and prayers she kissed him good-night and closed the door. Jamie frowned. He knew that he had not brushed hi teeth but he felt sleepy. He thought he would just rest for a while and then get up to brush his teeth. But Jamie's eyes closed.

"Brush, brush, brush your teeth,
Brush them how they grow,
Down on those from up above,
Up on those below."

Who was singing? Jamie saw shadows. Giant tooth brushes seemed to be dancing at his window.

"Brush, brush, brush your teeth,
Brush them how they grow."
Tooth brushes marched across the bedroom wall.

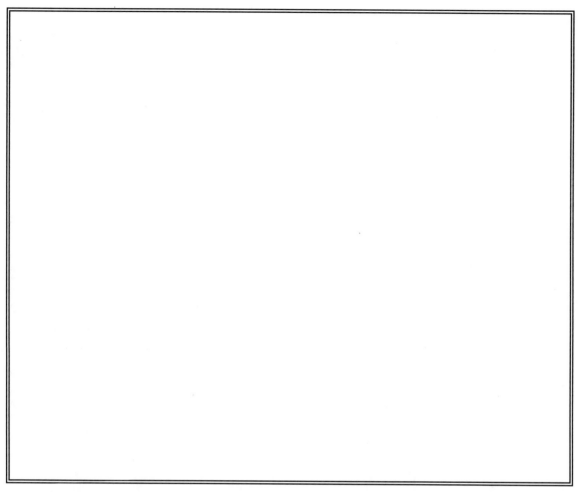

"Brush, brush, brush your teeth."

Tooth brushes jumped onto the bookcase and swung from the lamp.

"Brush, brush, brush your teeth."

Jamie's eyes flew open! He looked at the window but all he could see were the branches of the large tree swaying in the breeze. He looked at his wall. But all he could see were tiny tin soldiers on the wall paper. He looked at the lamp. But all he could see were his toy airplanes hanging from the lamp shade.

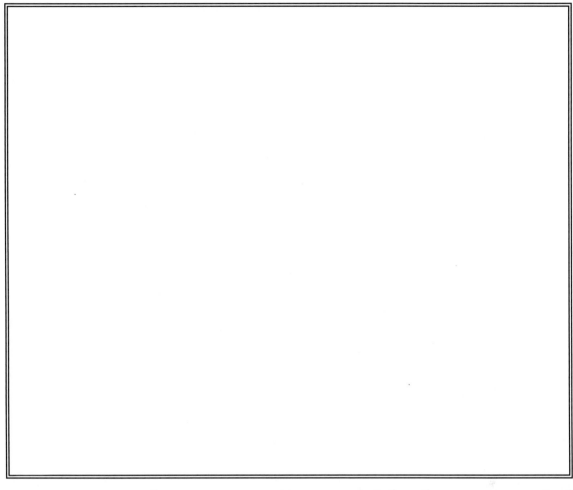

Very quietly Jamie got out of bed. He tiptoed across the hall to the bathroom and turned on the light. Very carefully he put some toothpaste onto his bright blue tooth brush and began to brush his teeth. In his mind he could still hear the tooth brushes singing.

Softly Jamie padded back across the hall and climbed into bed. Downstairs Mummy smiled and softly hummed a familiar tune.